HOW MAY WE CURE DISTRACTIONS IN HOLY DUTIES?

How May We Cure Distractions in Holy Duties?

REV. THOMAS MANTON D.D.
MINISTER OF THE WORD

CURIOSMITH

MINNEAPOLIS

Published by Curiosmith.
Minneapolis, Minnesota.
Internet: curiosmith.com.

Previously published as part of *The Morning-Exercise at Cripple-gate, or Several Cases of Conscience Practically Resolved by Sundry Ministers*. London: T. Milbourn, Joshua Johnson, 1661.

The text for this edition is: *The Morning Exercises at Cripplegate, St. Giles in the Fields and Southwark; etc.*, Vol. 2., James Nichols, edit., London: Thomas Tegg, 1844.

Unless otherwise stated, the notes and quotes in the footnotes are the original Greek and Latin notes translated into English by James Nichols (1785–1861). When a translation exists, Latin and Greek phrases are sometimes omitted for ease of reading.

Source of the biography: Samuel Dunn. *Memoirs of the Seventy-five Eminent Divines whose Discourses Form The Morning Exercises at Cripplegate, St. Giles in the Fields, and in Southwark.* London: John Snow, 1844.

Elizabethan verbs and pronouns are updated to modern English word for word.

The "Guide to the Contents" was added to this edition by the publisher.

ISBN 9781946145482

GUIDE TO THE CONTENTS

GUIDE TO THE CONTENTS *(Continued)*

Biographical Sketch of

Rev. Thomas Manton, D.D.

This truly excellent divine was born at Lawrence-Lydiat, Somersetshire, in 1620. His father, who was minister of Whimpole, after Thomas had made some considerable progress in his studies at the free school at Tiverton, placed him, when but fifteen years of age, at Wadham College, Oxford. From thence, in 1639, he was translated to Hart Hall, and took the degree of A.B. Before he was twenty he was ordained by the celebrated Bishop Hall, who at the time expressed his opinion, that he would be an extraordinary person. He entered on the ministry when the King and Parliament were in open hostility, and was confined to Exeter, when it was besieged by the king's forces. At Sowton near that city, he preached his first sermon from Matthew 7:1. About the year 1643, he was settled at Stoke Newington, to which living he was presented by the Hon. Colonel Popham, in whom he had a kind patron, and whose pious lady also highly esteemed him. He continued seven years at Newington, and there in his course of weekly lectures he went through his exposition of James and Jude, which he published. Being an excellent preacher, he was frequently invited to preach before the Parliament, and on other public occasions. A discourse on Deuteronomy 33:4, 5, which he delivered just after he had given his testimony against the death of Charles I, gave great offense, and some in the house talked of sending him to prison, but they refrained. About 1650, he succeeded the Rev. Obadiah Sedgwick as rector of Covent Garden. He was presented to this living by the Earl, afterwards Duke, of Bedford, who always very highly esteemed him. In 1651, Mr. Christopher Love, having been convicted of carrying on a secret correspondence with Charles II, was sentenced to be beheaded on Towerhill. Mr. Manton, who highly respected him, attended him to the scaffold, and resolved to preach his funeral sermon. At this the government expressed some displeasure, and the soldiers threatened to shoot him. He, however, was not to be terrified, but preached at Mr. Love's church in St. Lawrence Jewry, to a numerous congregation, and afterwards printed the sermon. When Cromwell attained the protectorship, in 1653, he sent for him to Whitehall, on the morning of his installment, and desired him to pray on the occasion. Mr. Manton requested to be excused, particularly urging the shortness of the notice, but Oliver replied, that such a man as he could not be at a loss to perform the service, and put him into his study for half an hour to premeditate. About the same time he became one of Cromwell's chaplains; he was nominated by Parliament on a committee of divines, to draw up a scheme of fundamentals, and on another committee, for examining and approving of ministers. In 1658, he assisted at the inauguration of Richard Cromwell to the protectorship, and in the following year was curator of the press, with Dr. Reynolds and Mr. Calamy. Dr. Harris relates the following anecdote of him: "Being called to preach before the Lord Mayor and Court of Aldermen at St. Paul's, he chose a subject in which he might display his learning. He received thanks for his performance. But as he was returning a poor man gently pulled the sleeve of his gown, and asked if he was not the gentleman who preached before the Lord Mayor. He replied, he was. 'Sir,' said the man, 'I came with an earnest desire after the Word of God, and in hope of getting some good to my soul, but I was greatly disappointed, for I could not understand a great deal of what you said—you were quite above me.' The Doctor replied with tears, 'Friend, if I did not give you a sermon, you have given me one; and by the grace of God, I will never play the fool to preach before my Lord Mayor, in such a manner again.'"

In 1660, Mr. Manton was very instrumental, with many other Presbyterian divines, in the restoration of Charles II. He was one of the ministers appointed to wait upon the King at Breda; and was afterwards sworn one of his Majesty's chaplains, though he never preached at Court. He was also, by the King's mandate, created doctor of divinity at Oxford; and soon after was offered the deanery of Rochester, which, on finding how things were going at Court, he refused. In 1661, he was one of the Commissioners at the Savoy conference, where he used his utmost endeavors for a reconciliation, but without success. After his ejectment on August 24, 1662, he preached on the Lord's Day evenings in his own house; and also on Wednesday mornings, when the violence of the times would permit. In 1670, he was apprehended on a Sabbath afternoon just as he had concluded his sermon, and in a few days after was committed to prison, where he continued six months; but received very gentle usage. After his release he preached in a large room in White Hart-yard, where on a Lord's Day morning a band came to seize him, but he escaped their fury. The place was fined forty pounds, and the minister twenty, which Lord Wharton, who was present, paid. In 1672, the merchants and other citizens of London, set up lectures on Tuesday morning, at Pinners' Hall; when Dr. Manton was one of the first six chosen, and opened the lecture.

When his health began to fail, he spent some time at Woburn with Lord Wharton, but finding little benefit by it, he returned to town. The day before he took his bed, he was in his study, of which he took a solemn leave with hands and eyes lift up to heaven, blessing God for the many comfortable and serious hours he had spent there, and waiting in joyful hope of a state of clearer knowledge, and higher enjoyments of God. At night he prayed with his family under great indisposition, and recommended himself to God's wise disposal; desiring, "If he had no further work for him to do in this world, he would take him to himself." He died October 18, 1677, in the fifty-seventh year of his age, and lies interred in the chancel of the church at Stoke Newington. He was of a middle stature, and of a fair and fresh complexion, with a great mixture of majesty and sweetness in his countenance. In his younger years he was very slender; but grew corpulent in his advanced age; not by idleness or excess, for he was remarkably temperate and unweariedly diligent, but by a sedentary life.

Dr. Bates, who had a most affectionate esteem for him, preached his funeral sermon, and says, "His name is worthy of precious and eternal memory. A clear judgment, a rich fancy, strong memory, and happy elocution met in him; and were excellently improved by his diligent study. He was endowed with an extraordinary knowledge of the Scripture.

His discourses were so clear and convincing, that none, without offering violence to conscience, could resist their evidence and from hence they were effectual, not only to inspire a sudden flame and raise a short commotion in the affections, but to make a lasting change in the life. His doctrine was uncorrupt and pure. He did not entertain his hearers with impertinent subtleties, empty notions, intricate disputes, dry and barren, without production of virtue; but as one who always had in his eye the great end of his ministry, the glory of God, and the salvation of men. His style was not exquisitely studied, not consisting of harmonious periods, but far distant from vulgar meanness. His expression was natural and free, clear, and eloquent, quick and powerful; without any spice of folly; and always suitable to the simplicity and majesty of divine truth. He abhorred a vain ostentation of wit in handling sacred truths, so venerable and grave, and of eternal consequence. His fervor and earnestness in preaching was such as might soften and make pliant the most stubborn and obstinate spirit. I am not speaking of one whose talent was only voice, who labored in the pulpit as if the end of preaching were the exercise of the body, and not the profit of souls. But this man was inflamed with holy zeal, and from thence such expressions broke forth as were capable of procuring attention and consent in his hearers. He spoke as one who had a living faith within him of divine truth. This faithful minister abounded in the work of the Lord; and, which is truly admirable, though so frequent in preaching, yet was always superior to others, and equal to himself. He was no fomenter of faction, but studious of the public tranquillity. Consider him as a Christian, his life was answerable to his doctrine. He was like a fruitful tree, which produces in the branches what it contains in the root. His inward grace was made visible in a conversation becoming the gospel. His resolute contempt of the world secured him from being wrought upon by those motives which tempt low spirits from their duty. His generous constancy of mind in resisting the current of popular humor, declared his loyalty to his Divine Master. His charity was eminent in procuring supplies for others, when in mean circumstances himself. He was deeply affected with the sense of his frailty and unworthiness."

In 1678, Dr. Bates published Manton's Twenty Sermons, in quarto, and gives the following account of them:—"The main design of them is to represent the inseparable connection between Christian duties and privileges, wherein the essence of our religion consists. The Gospel is not a naked, unconditionate offer of pardon and eternal life in favor of sinners, but upon the most convenient terms for the glory of God and the good of men, enforced by the strongest obligations upon them to receive humbly and thankfully those benefits. The Son of God came into the world, not to make God less holy, but to make us holy; and not to vacate our duty, and free us from the law as a rule of obedience, for that is both impossible and would be most infamous and reproachful to our Saviour. To challenge such an exemption in point of right is to make ourselves gods; to usurp it in point of fact, is to make ourselves devils."

In 1679 was published, in octavo, his Eighteen Sermons on the Second Chapter of the Second Epistle to the Thessalonians. In the preface to this volume, Baxter says of him, "How sound he was in judgment against extremes in the controversies of these times; how great a lamenter of the scandalous and deriding mistakes of some self-conceited men; how earnestly desirous of healing our present breaches, and not unacquainted with the proper means and terms; how hard and successful a student, how frequent and laborious a preacher; and how highly and deservedly esteemed, is commonly known here."

In 1684, Dr. Bates published his Exposition of the Lord's Prayer. In 1685, Mr. Hurst published his Discourses tending to promote Peace and Holiness among Christians; and Dr. Jacomb, Christ's Temptations and Transfiguration. In 1703 was published, A Practical Exposition of Isaiah 53. The Doctor wrote a preface to Case's Meditations; to

Smectymnuus; to Clifford's Book of the Covenant; to Ignatius Jourdain's Life; Strong's Sermons of the Certainty and Eternity of Hell Torments; and to the second edition, in quarto, of the Assembly's Confession of Faith.

Besides these lesser works, there are five large volumes in folio. The first was, Sermons upon the 119th Psalm. The second contains, Sermons on the 25th of Matthew, and 17th of John; the 6th and 8th of the Romans; and the 5th of the Second Epistle to the Corinthians. The third volume contains Sermons upon the 11th chapter to the Hebrews, with a Treatise of the Life of Faith, etc. The fourth contains Sermons upon several texts of Scripture. The fifth volume contains Sermons on the 5th to the Ephesians, on the 3rd of Philippians, on 2 Thessalonians 1, 1 John 3rd chapter, with one hundred and forty sermons on particular texts.

Dr. Manton was unquestionably one of the greatest divines of his own, or of any other age. Archbishop Usher said, "He was one of the best preachers in England;" and Charnock, "That he was the best collector of sense of the age;" and Waller the poet observed, "That he never discoursed with such a man as Dr. Manton in his life." He was faithful in reproving sin. Duke Lauderdale, who pretended to carry it with great respect for him, in some company where the Doctor was present, behaved himself very indecently: the Doctor modestly reproved him; but the Duke never loved him afterwards. He was once at dinner at Lord Manchester's, in Whitehall, when several persons of great note began to drink the King's health, a custom then in vogue, and which was commonly abused to great disorders. When it came to him he refused to comply with it, apprehending it beneath the dignity of a minister, to give any countenance to the sinful excess it so often occasioned. It put a stop to it at that time, and Prince Rupert, who was present, inquired who he was.

In the interval, between the Restoration and his ejectment, Manton was greatly esteemed by persons of the first quality at court, which, however, he improved, not for himself, but for others. The following instance is worth recording. Mr. James, of Berkshire, an honest and worthy person, was at the point of being cast out of his living. He came to London to make friends to the Lord Chancellor Hyde, but could find none proper for his purpose. He was at length advised to go to Dr. Manton, to whom he was yet a stranger. It was late in the evening, when the Doctor was in bed. He told his case to Mrs. Manton, who advised him to come again in the morning. He answered, with great concern, that it would be too late, and that if he could not put a stop to it that night, he and his family must be ruined. On so pressing a case the Doctor rose, and went with him to the Lord Chancellor, at

York-house, who, spying the Doctor in the crowd, called to him to know what business he had there at that time of night. When he acquainted him with his errand, my lord called to the person who stamped the orders upon such occasions, and asked him what he was doing? He answered, "That he was just going to put the stamp to an order for passing away such a living." Upon which he bid him stop; and told the Doctor his friend should not be molested.

Upon a public fast in Covent Garden church, for the persecuted Protestants in the valleys of Piedmont, Dr. Manton had got Mr. Baxter and Dr. Wilkins to assist him. Baxter commenced, and preached on Amos 6:6, "But they are not grieved for the afflictions of Joseph." He, after his manner, took a great compass, and grasped the whole subject. Manton succeeded him, and had chosen the same text; he was obliged often to refer to the former discourse, and to say every now and then, "As it has been observed by my reverend brother." Dr. Wilkins sat very uneasy, and reckoned that between them both, he should have nothing left to say; for he had fixed upon the same text too. He insisted upon being excused, but Dr. Manton obliged him to go up into the pulpit, and by an ingenious artifice he succeeded admirably. Before he named his text, he prepared the audience, by expressing his fears of their narrow-spiritedness and little concern for the interest of God in the world; for, says he, "without any knowledge or design of our own, we have all three been directed to the same words;" which, spoken with the majesty and authority peculiar to the presence and spirit of that excellent person, so awakened the attention and disposed the minds of the people, that he was heard with more regard, and was thought to do more good, than both the former, though he had scarce a single thought throughout the sermon distinct from the other two. Dr. Manton's sermons in the Morning Exercises are:—How may we cure distractions in holy duties?—How to improve our baptism.—Man's impotency to keep himself out of misery.—The Scripture a sufficient rule of Christian faith.

HOW MAY WE CURE DISTRACTIONS IN HOLY DUTIES?

by Rev. Thomas Manton, D.D.

Ye hypocrites, well did Esaias prophesy of you, saying, This people draweth nigh unto me with their mouth, and honoureth me with their lips; but their heart is far from me.—MATTHEW 15:7, 8.

In this chapter you will find a contest between Christ and the Pharisees, about their traditions and old customs, which they valued above the commandments of God, as it is usual with formal men to love chains of their own making, and to make conscience of a tradition when yet they can dispense with a commandment; and thereby discovering themselves to be very hypocrites, who are more in externals than in internals, in show than substance, minding the formality rather than the spirit and life of service to God. Our Lord confirms his censure by the testimony of the prophet Isaiah, "Ye hypocrites," etc.

I shall not stand explaining the words. *Drawing*

nigh—Is a phrase peculiar to worship, especially to invocation. *Mouth and lips*—Are put for all external gestures, and that bodily exercise which is necessary to the worship of God, especially for words. *But their heart is far from me*—It chiefly intends their habitual averseness from God, but may also comprise the wandering and roving of the mind in duty, which is a degree and spece[1] of it. Of that I shall treat at this time; and my note will be—

That distraction of thoughts, or the removing of the heart from God in worship, is a great sin, and [a] degree of hypocrisy.

The text speaks of gross hypocrisy, or a zealous pretence of outward worship without any serious bent of heart towards God. But any removal of the heart from him in times necessary to think of him, is a degree of it; for though distractions in worship are incident to the people of God, yet they are culpable, and do so far argue the relics of hypocrisy in them. I shall show—

I. The GREATNESS of the sin.

II. The CAUSES.

III. The REMEDIES.

I. That there is such a sin, sad experience witnesses: vain thoughts intrude importunately upon the soul in every duty. In hearing the Word we are

---

1 This word is printed *spece, speice,* and *spice,* in the different editions; but *spece,* the reading of the first, is proper, signifying "a sample, a specimen."—Nichols.

not free;[1] nor in singing; but chiefly they haunt us in prayer; and, of all kinds of prayer, in mental prayer, when our addresses to God are managed by thoughts alone, there we are more easily disturbed. Words bound the thoughts, and the inconvenience of an interruption is more sensible, as occasioning a pause in our speech; and as in mental prayer, so when we join with others, to keep time and pace with their words, (unless the Lord quicken them to an extraordinary liveliness,) we find it very hard. But how GREAT a Sin this is, is my first task to show. I shall do it,

1. By three *general* considerations.

2. By speaking *particularly* to the present case.

1. *Generally.*

(1.) *Consider how tender God is of his worship.*—He has said, that he "will be sanctified in all that draw nigh unto him."[2] *To sanctify* is "to set apart from common use." Now, God will be sanctified; that is, not treated with as an ordinary person, but with special heedfulness of soul and affection becoming so great a Majesty. When you think to put him off with any thing, you lessen his excellency and greatness, and do not sanctify him, or glorify him as God; and therefore God pleads his Majesty when they would put a sorry sacrifice upon him, as if every thing were good enough for him.

1 Ezekiel 33:31.

2 Leviticus 10:3.

"Cursed be the deceiver, which hath in his flock a male, and voweth, and sacrificeth unto the Lord a corrupt thing: for I am a great King, saith the Lord of hosts."[1] To be slight in his service argues mean thoughts of God. "Be not rash with thy mouth, and let not thine heart be hasty to utter any thing before God: for God is in heaven, and thou upon earth."[2] We forget our distance, and by a bold profaneness are too fellow-like and familiar with God, when we are not deeply serious and exact in what we do and say in his presence, but only babble over a few impertinent words without attention and affection. Certainly, God is very sensible of the wrong and contempt we put upon him; for he notes "All things are naked and opened unto the eyes of Him with whom we have to do."[3] And he will not put it up;[4] for he tells us, that he "will not hold him guiltless that taketh his name in vain;"[5] and he will be as good as his word; for the least disorders in worship have been sorely punished: witness the stroke from heaven upon Aaron's sons;[6] the breach made upon Uzzah;[7] and the havoc made

---

1 Malachi 1:14.

2 Ecclesiastes 5:2.

3 Hebrews 4:13.

4 This is an old form of English speech, tantamount in meaning to its cognate, *not to put up with it*, "not to endure it without expressions of anger or dissatisfaction."—NICHOLS.

5 Exodus 20:7.

6 Leviticus 10:2.

7 2 Samuel 6:7.

of the Beth-shemites;[1] the diseases that raged at Corinth.[2] And though judgments be not so rife and visible now upon our unhallowed approaches to God, yet he smites us with *deadness* where he does not smite us with *death:* for a man is punished otherwise than a boy; and judgments are now spiritual, which, in the infancy of the church, were temporal and bodily. Certainly, we have all cause to tremble when we come before the Lord.

(2.) *The more sincere anyone is, the more he makes conscience of his thoughts.*—Is more observant of them, and more troubled about them. "Let the unrighteous man forsake his thoughts," etc.[3] Then he begins to be serious, and to have a conscience indeed when his thoughts trouble him. So David: "I hate vain thoughts: but thy law do I love."[4] We think thoughts are free and subject to no tribunal. If there be any error in them, we think it is a very venial one. They betray us to no shame in the world, and therefore we let them go without dislike and remorse. But a child of God cannot pass over the matter so; he knows that thoughts are the immediate births of the soul, and do much discover the temper of it; that there actions begin; and if "vain thoughts" be suffered to lodge in him, he

---

1 1 Samuel 6:19.
2 1 Corinthians 11:30.
3 Isaiah 55:7.
4 Psalm 119:113.

will soon fall into further mischief; and therefore he considers what he *thinks*, as well as what he *speaks* and *does:* and if at all times, especially in worship, where the workings of the inward man are of chief regard, and the acts of the outward only required as a help to our serving God "in the spirit."[1]

(3.) *Carelessness in duties is the high way to atheism.*—For every formal and slight prayer hardens the heart, and make way for contempt of God. Men that have made bold with God in duty, and it succeeds well with them—their awe of God is lessened, and the lively sense of his glory and majesty abated, till it be quite lost: by degrees they outgrow all feelings and tenderness of conscience; every time you come to God slightly, you lose ground by coming, till at length you look upon worship as a mere custom, or something done for fashion's sake.

2. *Particularly.*

(1.) *It is an affront to God, and a kind of mockery.*—We wrong his Omnisciency, as if he saw not the heart, and could not tell man his thought. It is God's essential glory in worship to be acknowledged an all-seeing "Spirit," and accordingly to be worshipped "in spirit and in truth."[2] Thoughts are as audible with him as words; therefore, when you prattle words, and do not make conscience of thoughts, you do not worship him as a Spirit.

---

1 Philippians 3:3.
2 John 4:24.

We wrong his Majesty when we speak to him in prayer, and do not give heed to what we say. Surely, we are not to prattle, like jays or parrots, words without affection and feeling; or to chatter like cranes; or be like Ephraim, whom the prophet calls "a silly dove without a heart." A mean man takes it ill when you have business to talk with him about, and your minds are elsewhere; you would all judge it to be an affront to the Majesty of God, if a man should send his clothes stuffed with straw, or a puppet dressed up, instead of himself, into the assemblies of God's people, and think this should supply his personal presence; yet our clothes stuffed with straw, or an image dressed up instead of us, (such as Michal put into David's bed)[1] would be less offensive to God than our bodies without our souls. The absence of the spirit is the absence of the more noble part. We pretend to speak to God, and do not hear ourselves, nor can give any account of what we pray for. Or rather let me give you Chrysostom's comparison: A man would have been thought to have profaned the mysteries of the Levitical worship, if, instead of sweet incense, he should put into the censer sulphur or brimstone, or mingle the one with the other.[2] Surely, our prayers should be "set forth as incense."[3] And do not we affront God to his face, that mingle

---

1 1 Samuel 19:12, 13.
2 CHRYSOSTOM *Homil. 74 in Matt.*
3 Psalm 141:2.

so many vain, sinful, proud, filthy, blasphemous thoughts? What is this but to mingle sulphur with our incense? Again: when God speaks to us, and knocks at the heart, and there is none within to hear him, is it not an affront to his Majesty? Put it in a temporal case: If a great person should talk to us, and we should neglect him, and entertain ourselves with his servants, he would take it as a despite and contempt done to him. The great God of heaven and earth does often call you together to speak to you. Now, if you think so slightly of his speeches as not to attend, but set your minds adrift, to be carried hither and thither with every wave, where is that reverence [which] you owe to him?

It is a wrong to his Goodness, and the comforts of his holy presence; for, in effect, you say that you do not find that sweetness in God which you expect, and therefore are weary of his company before your business be over with him. It is said of the Israelites, when they were going for Canaan, that "in their hearts they turned back again into Egypt."[1] They had more mind to be in Egypt than under Moses's government, and their thoughts ever ran upon the flesh-pots and belly-cheer [which] they enjoyed there. We are offended with their impatience and murmurings, and the affronts they put upon their guides; and do not we even the same and worse in our careless manner of worshipping? When God

1 Acts 7:39.

has brought us into his presence, we do in effect say, "Give us the world again: this is better entertainment for our thoughts than God and holy things." If Christians would but interpret their actions, they would be ashamed of them. Is any thing more worthy to be thought of than God? The Israelites' hearts were upon Egypt in the wilderness; and our hearts are upon the world, nay, every toy, even when we are at the throne of grace, and conversing with Him who is the center of our rest, and the fountain of our blessedness.

(2.) *It grieves the Spirit of God.*—He is grieved with our vain thoughts, as well as [with] our scandalous actions. Other sins may shame us more; but these are a grief to the Spirit, because they are conceived in the heart, which is his presence-chamber, and place of special residence. And he is most grieved with these vain thoughts which haunt us in the time of our special addresses to God, because his peculiar operations are hindered, and the heart is set open to God's adversary in God's presence, and the world and Satan are suffered to interpose in the very time of the reign of grace, then when it should be *in solio*, "in its royalty," commanding all our faculties to serve it. This is to steal away the soul from under Christ's own arm. As a captain of a garrison is troubled when the enemies come to prey under the very walls, in the face of all his forces and strength; so, certainly, it is a grief to the

Spirit when our lusts have power to disturb us in holy duties, and the heart is taken up with unclean glances, and worldly thoughts, then when we present ourselves before the Lord. God looks upon his people's sins as aggravated, because committed in his own house: "In my house have I found their wickedness."[1] What is this but to dare God to his very face? Solomon saith, "A king that sitteth in the throne of judgment scattereth away all evil with his eyes."[2] They are bold men that dare break the laws when a magistrate is upon the throne, and actually exercising judgment against offenders: so it argues much impudence, that when we come to deal with God, as sitting upon the throne, and observing and looking upon us, that we can yet lend our hearts to our lusts, and suffer every vain thought to divert us. There is more of modesty, though little of sincerity, in them that say to their lusts, as Abraham to his servants: "Abide ye here; and I will go yonder and worship;"[3] or, as they say, the serpent lays aside her poison when she goes to drink. When a man goes to God, he should leave his lusts behind him; not for a while, and with an intent to entertain them again, but for ever. However, this argues some reverence of God, and sense of the weight of holy duties; but when we bring them along with us, it is a sign we

1 Jeremiah 23:11.
2 Proverbs 20:8.
3 Genesis 22:5.

little mind the work we go about.

(3.) *It is a spiritual disease.*—The soul has its diseases as well as the body. The unsteady roving of the mind, or the disturbance of vain and impertinent thoughts, is one of those diseases. Shall I call it a *spiritual madness*, or *fever*, or *shaking palsy*, or all these? You know, mad men make several relations, and rove from one thing to another, and are gone off from a sentence ere they have well begun it: our thoughts are as slippery and inconsistent as their speeches; therefore what is this but the frenzy of the soul? What mad creatures would we seem to be, if all our thoughts were patent, or an invisible notary were lurking in our hearts to write them down! We run from object to object in a moment, and one thought looks like a mere stranger upon another; we wander and run through all the world in an instant. O, who can count the numberless operations and workings of our mind in one duty? What impertinent excursions have we from things good to lawful, from lawful to sinful, from ordinarily sinful to downright blasphemous! Should any one of us, after he has been some time exercised in duty, go aside and write down his thoughts, and the many interlinings of his own prayers, he would stand amazed at the madness and light discurrency of his own imaginations.

Or shall I call it *the feverish distemper of the soul? Ægri somnia* ["the dreams of a sick man"] is a proverb. In fevers men have a thousand fancies and swimming toys in their dreams; and just so it is with our souls in God's worship. We bring that curse upon us spiritually, which corporally God threatened to bring upon the Jews: "I will scatter you to the end of the earth." We scatter our thoughts hither and thither, without any consistency. The heart, in regard of this roving madness, is like a runagate servant, who, when he has left his master, wanders up and down, and knows not where to fix; or like those that are full of distracting business, that cannot make a set meal, but take their diet by snatches.

(4.) *It argues the loss and non-acceptance of our prayers.*—You are in danger to lose your worship, at least so much of it as you do not attend upon. And, truly, to a man that knows the value of that kind of traffic, this is a very great loss. You that are tradesmen are troubled if you happen to be abroad when a good customer comes to deal with you. The ordinances of God are the market for your souls: if you had not been abroad, with Esau, you might have received the blessing, and gone away richly loaden from a prayer, from the Word, and the Lord's Supper; but you lose your advantages for want of attention. Allowed distractions turn your prayers into sin, and make them no prayers. When the soul departs from the body, it is no longer a man, but a carcass: so when the thoughts are gone from prayer, it is no longer a prayer; the essence of the duty is wanting. What is prayer? Ἀνάβασις τοῦ νοῦ, as Damascene defined it, "The lifting up of the heart to God." Many have prayed *without words;* but never any prayed *without lifting up* or *pouring out the heart.* If a man should kneel, and use a gesture of worship, and fall asleep, no doubt that man does not pray. This is to sleep with the heart, and the words uttered are but like a dream, have but a slight touch of reason in them, a mere drowsy, unattentive devotion. The soul is asleep, though the eyes be not closed, and the senses locked up. Can we expect that God should hear us and bless us because of our mere outward presence? We are ashamed of those that sleep at a duty; and this is as bad or worse: they may sleep out of natural infirmity, as weakness, age, sickness, etc.; but this does more directly proceed from some slightness or irreverence. Well, then, with what face can we expect the fruit of that prayer to which we have not attended? "It is a great presumption to desire God to hear those requests, a great part whereof we have not heard ourselves: if they be not worthy of our attention, they are far more unworthy of God's." Cyprian, or Ruffinus, or whoever was the author of the explication of the Lord's Prayer in Cyprian's works, has a notable passage to this purpose: "Thou art unmindful of thyself, thou dost not hear thyself; and how canst thou with reason desire the blessing and comfort of the duty which thou thoughtest not worthy thine own attention and regard?"[1]

I would not willingly grate too hard upon a tender conscience: it is a question that is often propounded, "Whether wandering thoughts do altogether frustrate a duty, and make it of none effect;" and "whether, in some case, a virtual attention does not suffice." There is an *actual* intention, and a *virtual* intention. The *actual* intention is when a soul does distinctly and constantly regard every thing that is said and done in a duty; and a *virtual* intention is, when we keep only a disposition and purpose to attend, though many times we fail and are carried aside. This Aquinas calls *primam intentionem;* ["the first intention;"] out of the Scripture we may call it, the "setting of the heart and soul to seek the Lord."[2] Now, what shall we say in this case? On the one side, we must not be too strict, lest we prejudice the comfort and expectation of God's people. When did they ever manage a duty but they are guilty of some wanderings? It is much to keep up our hearts to the main and solid requests that are made to God in prayer. But, on the other side, we must not be too remiss, lest we encourage indiligence and careless devotion. Briefly, then, by way

1 *"Quomodo te a Deo exaudiri postulas, cum te ipse non audias? Vis Deum esse memorem tui cum rogas, cum ipse tui memor non sis?"*—CYPRIAN *De Oratione Dominicá.*
2 1 Chronicles 22:19.

of answer, there is a threefold distraction in prayer, *distractio invita, negligens, et voluntaria.*

(1.) There is *distractio invita*, "an unwilling distraction."—When the heart is seriously and solemnly set to seek God, and yet we are carried beside our purpose; for it is impossible so to shut doors and windows but that some wind will get in; so to guard the heart as to be wholly free from vain thoughts; but they are not constant, frequent, allowed, but resisted, prayed against, striven against, bewailed; and then they are not iniquities, but infirmities, which the Lord will pardon. He will gather up the broken parts of our prayers, and in mercy give us an answer. I say, where this distraction is retracted with grief, resisted with care, as Abraham drove away the fowls, when they came to pitch upon his sacrifice;[1] it is to be reckoned among the infirmities of the saints, which do not hinder their consolation.

(2.) There is *distractio negligens*, "a negligent distraction."—When a man has an intention to pray, and express his desires to God, but he prays carelessly, and does not guard his thoughts; so that sometimes he wanders, and sometime recovers himself again, and then strays again, and is in and out, off and on, with God; as a spaniel[2] roves up and down, and is still crossing the ways, sometimes

---

1 Genesis 15:11.

2 Spaniel—a mean, cringing, fawning person. *(Webster's 1828 Dictionary.)*

losing the company he goes with, and then retiring to them again. I cannot say, this man prays not at all, or that God does not hear him; but he will have little comfort in his prayers; yea, if he be serious, they will minister more matter of grief to him than comfort; and therefore he ought to be more earnest and sedulous in resisting this infirmity, that he may be assured of audience: otherwise, if his heart be not affected with it in time, by degrees all those motions and dispositions of heart that are necessary to prayer will be eaten out and lost.

(3.) There is *distractio voluntaria*, "a voluntary distraction."—When men mind no more than the task or work wrought, and only go round in a track of accustomed duties, without considering with what heart they perform them—this is such a vanity of mind as turns the whole prayer into sin.

II. The CAUSES of this roving and impertinent intrusion of vain thoughts.

1. *Satan is one cause*, who does *maxime insidiari orationibus*, as Cassian speaks, "lie in wait to hinder the prayers of the saints."—Whenever we minister before the Lord, he is at our right hand ready to resist us.[1] And therefore the apostle James, when he bids us "draw nigh to God," bids us also to "resist the devil;"[2] implying thereby, that there is no drawing nigh to God without resisting Satan.

---

1 Zechariah 3:1.

2 James 4:7, 8.

When a tale is told, and you are going about the affairs of the world, he does not trouble you; for these things do not trouble him, or do any prejudice to his kingdom. But when you are going to God, and that in a warm, lively, affectionate manner, he will be sure to disturb you, seeking to abate the edge of your affections, or divert your minds. Formal prayers pattered over do him no harm; but when you seriously set yourselves to call upon God, he says within himself, "This man will pray *for God's glory;* and then I am at a loss; *for the coming of Christ's kingdom*, and then mine goes to wreck; *that God's will may be done upon earth as it is in heaven*, and that minds me of my old fall; and my business is to cross the will of God. He will pray *for daily bread*, and that strengthens dependence; for *pardon* and *comfort*, and then I lose ground; for the devils are the 'rulers of the darkness of this world.'[1] He will pray *to be kept from sin and temptation;* and that is against me." Thus Satan is afraid of the prayers of the saints; he is concerned in every request you make to God; and therefore he will hinder or cheat you of your prayers; if you will needs be praying, he will carry away your hearts. Now, much he can do, if you be not watchful; he can present objects to the senses which stir up thoughts, yea, pursue his temptations, and cast in one fiery dart after another; therefore we had need

1 Ephesians 6:12.

stand upon our guard.

2. *The natural levity of our spirits.*—Man is a restless creature. We have much ado to stay our hearts for any space of time in one state, much more in holy things, from which we are naturally averse: "When I would do good," το κακὸν ϖαράκειται, "evil is present with me."[1] O consider this natural feebleness of mind, whereby we are unable to keep long to any employment, but are light, feathery, tossed up and down like a dried leaf before the wind, or as an empty vessel upon the waves! It is so with us in most businesses, especially in those which are sacred. The apostle bids us "pray without ceasing;" and we cannot do it whilst we pray. He is a stranger to God and his own heart, who finds it not daily. This is an incurable vanity; though we often repent of it, yet it is not amended; a misery that God would leave upon our natures, to humble us while we are in the world, and that we may long for heaven. The angels and blessed spirits there are not troubled with those things: in heaven there is no complaining of wandering thoughts; there God is "all in all." They that are *there* have but one object to fill their understandings, one object to give contentment to their desires; their hearts cleave to God inseparably by a perfect love; but *here* we are cumbered with much serving; and much work begets a multitude of thoughts in us. "The Lord knoweth the thoughts

1 Romans 7:21.

of man, that they are vanity."[1] When we have summed up all the traverses, reasonings, and discourses of the mind, we may write at the bottom this, as the total sum: "Here is nothing but vanity."

3. *Another cause is practical atheism.*—We have little sense of things that are unseen and lie within the veil, in the world of spirits. Things that are seen have a great force upon us. "Offer it now unto thy governor," says the prophet.[2] God is afar off, both from our sight and apprehension; senses bind attention. If you speak to a man, your thoughts are settled, and you think of nothing else; but in speaking to God, you have not like attention, because you see him not. "Make us gods, which shall go before us:"[3] ay, that we would have a visible god, whom we may see and hear: but, the true God being a Spirit and an invisible Power, all the service that we do him is a task performed more out of custom than affection, in a slight, perfunctory way.

4. *Strong and unmortified lusts.*—Which being rooted in us, and having the soul at most command, will trouble us, and distract us when we go about any duty. Each man has a mind, and can spend it unweariedly as he is inclined, either to covetousness, ambition, or sensuality; for "where

---

1 Psalm 94:11.

2 Malachi 1:8.

3 Exodus 32:1.

the treasure is, there will the heart be also."[1] Set but the covetous man about the world, the voluptuous man about his pleasures, and the ambitious man about his honors and preferments; and will they suffer their thoughts to be taken off? Surely, no. But set either of these about holy things, and presently these lusts will be interposing. "Their heart goeth after their covetousness."[2] The sins to which a man is most addicted will engross the thoughts; so that this is one sign by which a man may know his reigning sin, that which interrupts him most in holy duties; for when all other lusts are kept out, Satan will be sure to set the darling sin a-work to plead for him. If a man be addicted to the world, so will his musings be; if to mirth, and good cheer, and vain sports, his thoughts will be taken up about them; if to the inordinate love of women, his fancy will be rolling upon carnal beauty, and he will be firing his heart with unclean thoughts.

5. *Want of love to God and holy things.*—Men are loath to come into God's presence for want of faith, and to keep there for want of love. Love fixes the thoughts, and dries up those swimming toys and fancies that do distract us. We ponder and muse upon that in which we delight. Were our natural hatred of God and of the means of grace changed into a perfect love, we should adhere

1 Matthew 6:21.
2 Ezekiel 33:31.

to him without distraction. We see, where men love strongly, they are deaf and blind to all other objects; they can think and speak of no other thing. But because our love to God is weak, every vain occasion carries away our minds from him. You find this by daily experience; when your affections flag in an ordinance, your thoughts are soon scattered; weariness makes way for wandering; our hearts are first gone, and then our minds. You complain you have not a settled mind; the fault is, you have not a settled love; for that would cause you to pause upon things without weariness. "His delight is in the law of the Lord; and in his law doth he meditate day and night."[1] "O how I love thy law! it is my meditation all the day."[2] David's mind would never run upon the Word so much, if his heart were not there. Thoughts are at the command and beck of love: where love bids them go, they go; and where love bids them tarry, they tarry; the saints first delight, and then meditate.

6. *Slightness and irreverence, or want of a sense of God's presence.*—A careless spirit will surely wander; but one deeply affected, is fixed and intent. Jonah, when he prayed in the whale's belly—could he have a heart to forget his work? Daniel, when he prayed among the lions—could he mind any thing else? When we are serious, and pray in good

---

1 Psalm 1:2.
2 Psalm 119:97.

earnest, we will call-in all our thoughts, and hold them under command. This question was put to Basil—how a man should keep the mind free from distraction: his answer was, that is, that "this evil came from slightness of heart, and unbelief of God's presence; for if a man did believe that God were before his eyes, searching the heart, and trying the reins, he would be serious."[1] "All things are naked and opened to Him with whom we have to do." God looks on, and so do the angels. He looks on the heart, and will not you be serious? Scholars that have a truant mind—yet the presence of their masters forces them to their books—the great God who tells man his thought—he sees. Our desires and thoughts speak louder in his ears than our words: therefore, possess the heart with a dread of his glorious presence, and with the weight and importance of the work we are about. Were we to deal with another man in a case of life and death, we would weigh our words, and not rove like madmen.

7. *The curiosity of the senses.*—These occasion a diversion. It is the office of the fancy to present, as in a glass, whatsoever is received by the external senses, or offered by the memory; and so the understanding takes notice of it. The wandering eye causes a wandering heart. Solomon says, "The

---

1 "γίγνεται ὁ μετεώρισμος ἀπὸ τῆς ἀργίας του νου, καὶ ἐξ ἀπιστίας μη ϖαρειναι τὸν θεὸν ἐξετάζοντα καρδίας καὶ νέφρους."—BASILIUS *in Regulis brevioribus.*

eyes of a fool are in the ends of the earth."[1] First his eyes rove, and then his heart. The apostle Peter says of unclean persons, that they have "eyes full of adultery;" μοιχαλιδος, "of the adulteress," as the word signifies.[2] The eye is rolled upon the object, and then the dart by the fancy is transmitted to the heart. Senses are the windows and doors of the soul: keep the senses, if you would keep the heart. Job was at a severe appointment with his eyes.[3] It is good when we go to God to renew these covenants; *to agree with the heart*, that we will not go to God without it; *with the eyes and ears*, that we will not see and hear any thing but what concerns our work. It was a strange constancy and fixedness which Josephus speaks of, when Faustus, Cornelius, and Furius, and Fabius, with their troops, had broken into the city of Jerusalem, and some fled one way and some another; yet the priests went on with their sacrifices and the holy rites of the temple, as if they heard nothing: though they rushed on them with their swords, yet they preferred the duty of their religion before their own safety.[4] And strange is that other instance of the Spartan youth, in Plutarch, that held the censer to Alexander whilst he was sacrificing; and though a coal lighted upon his flesh, he

---

1 Proverbs 17:24.

2 2 Peter 2:14.

3 Job 31:1.

4 JOSEPHUS *De Bellis Judæorum*.

suffered it to burn there, rather than, by any cry-
ing out, he would disturb the rites of their heathen-
ish superstition. Certainly these instances should
shame us Christians, that do not hold the senses
under a more severe restraint, but upon every light
occasion suffer them to trouble and distract us in
worship.

8. *Carking and distrustful cares.*—When we
are torn in pieces with the cares of the world, we
cannot have a composed heart; but our minds will
waver, and our dangers will recur to our thoughts,
and hinder the exercise of our faith. God took special care of the Jews, when they went up to worship,
that they might have nothing to trouble them; and
therefore he says, "The nations shall not desire thy
land, when thou shalt go up to appear before the
Lord thy God thrice in the year;"[1] and Augustine
gives the reason of it: "Lest they should be distracted
with thoughts about their own preservation," *vult
Deus intelligi ut securus quisque ascenderet, nec de
terrâ suâ sollicitus esset, Deo promittente custodi-
am.*[2] And one of the arguments by which Paul com-
mends single life, is freedom from the incumbrances

---

1 Exodus 34:24.

2 "God wished them to understand, that they might (each
of them) go up to the holy city with perfect security, devoid
of all solicitude respecting their land; for He promised to become its Guardian in their absence."—AUGUSTINE, *Quæst.*
161 *in Exod. (Nichols' trans.)*

of the world: "That ye may attend upon the Lord without distraction."[1]

REMEDIES

III. I might speak many things, by way of mere counsel, about guarding the senses, the use and abuse of a form, etc.; but all these are but like external applications in physic, or topical medicines, as the binding of things to the wrists of the hands, etc., which work no perfect cure of a disease, unless the distemper be purged away. Therefore I shall speak to those things that are most effectual.

1. *Go to God, and wait for the power of his grace.*—David, speaking of it as his work, [says,] "Unite my heart to fear thy name;"[2] fix it, gather it together. ἕνωσον τὴν καρδίαν μου, saith the Septuagint, "Make it one." The heart is multiplied when it is distracted by several thoughts. God has our hearts in his own hand; and when we can keep them up no longer, then he holds them up; when he withdraws his grace, we lose our life and seriousness. As meteors hang in the air as long as the heat of the sun is great, but when the sun is gone down they fall: as long as the love of God and the work of his grace are powerful in us, we are kept in a lively, heavenly frame; but as that abates, the soul swerves, and returns to vanity and sin. We read, that "the Lord

---

1 1 Corinthians 7:35.
2 Psalm 86:11.

opened the heart of Lydia, that she attended unto the things which were spoken of Paul."[1] *Attention* there bears somewhat a larger sense than we now consider it in; namely, "a deep regard to the doctrine of life;" yet this sense of fixedness of spirit cannot be excluded. Go to God, then; pray him to keep your heart together: he that has set bounds to the sea, and can bind up the waves in a heap, and stop the sun in its flight—certainly He can fasten and establish your heart and keep it from running out.

2. *Meditate on the greatness of Him before whom we are.*—It is of great consequence in duties to consider whom we take to be our party, "with whom we have to do."[2] In the word, God is the party that speaks to us: "Thou shalt be as my mouth;"[3] "As though God did beseech you by us."[4] It is God [that] speaks; and the heathen king of Moab showed such reverence, that when Ehud said, "I have a message from God unto thee, he arose out of his seat."[5] So in prayer, you have to do with God; you do as really minister before him as the angels that abide in his presence. O, if you could see Him that is invisible, you would have more reverence! A man that is praying or worshipping should behave himself as if he were in heaven, immediately

1 Acts 16:14.
2 Hebrews 4:13.
3 Jeremiah 15:19.
4 2 Corinthians 5:20.
5 Judges 3:20.

before God, in the midst of all the blessed angels, those "ten thousand times ten thousand" that stand before God. O, with what reverence, with what fear, should a poor worm creep into his presence![1] Think, then, of that glorious, all-seeing God, with whom you can converse *in thoughts,* as freely as with men *in words.* He knows all that is in your heart, and sees you through and through. If you had spoken all those things you have thought upon, you would be odious to men. If all our blasphemy, uncleanness, worldly projects, were known to those that join with us, should we be able to hold up our heads for blushing? And does not the Lord see all

---

1 "At the time of prayer, it is our paramount duty to enter into the very court of heaven; even into that court in which the King of Kings is seated on his high and starry throne, encircled with an innumerable and indescribable army of blessed spirits; which when he who saw them attempted to enumerate, his mental powers could furnish him with no higher numerical expressions than these: '*Thousand thousands* ministered unto Him, and *ten thousand times ten thousand* stood before Him!' (Daniel 7:10.) With what profound reverence, therefore, with what great awe, and deep humility, ought a vile and crawling frog to emerge from its muddy pond, and to approach into such an august and overpowering Presence! And how trembling and suppliant, how humble and anxious, while gazing with all the intensity of his spirit on the majesty of the Divine glory, will he who thus feels himself to be a mean 'worm and no man' be able to stand within the angelic circle, 'in the assembly of the upright, and in the congregation!' (Psalm 111:1.)"—BERNARDUS *De quatuor Modis orandi. (Nichols' trans.)*

this? Could we believe his inspection of the heart, there would be a greater awe upon us.

3. *Mortify those lusts that are apt to withdraw our minds.*—He that indulges any one vile affection will never be able to pray aright. Every duty will give you experience what corruption to resist. What thoughts are we haunted and pestered with, when we come to God? God requires prayer, that we may be weary of our lusts, and that the trouble that we find from them in holy exercises may exasperate our souls against them. We are angry with an importunate beggar, that will not be satisfied with any reasonable terms, but is always obtruding upon us. Every experience in this kind should give us an advantage to free our hearts from this disturbance. The whole work of grace tends to prayer; and the great exercise and employment of the spiritual life is, "watching unto prayer,"[1] and that prayer be not interrupted.[2]

4. *Before the duty there must be an actual preparation or a solemn discharge of all impediments, that we may not bring the world along with us.*— "Put off thy shoes from off thy feet," says God to Moses; "for the place whereon thou standest is holy ground."[3] Surely we should put off our carnal distractions when we go about holy duties. "Gird up

---

1 Ephesians 6:18.

2 1 Peter 3:7.

3 Exodus 3:5.

the loins of your mind," says the apostle Peter;[1] an allusion to long garments worn in that country. It is dangerous to come to prayer with a loose heart. "My heart is fixed," says David, "O God, my heart is fixed;"[2] that is, fitted, prepared, bended to God's worship. The soul must be set, put into a dexterous, ready posture. "There must be a resolved shutting of the heart against God's enemy, [and the opening of it only to God, in the hour of prayer,] lest he insinuate with us, and withdraw our minds."[3]

5. *Be severe to your purpose.*—And see that you regard nothing but what the duty leads you unto. It is the devil's policy to cheat us of the present duty by an unseasonable interposition. Satan begins with us in good things, that he may draw us to worse. What is unseasonable is naught. Watch against the first diversion, how plausible soever; it is an intruding thought that breaks a rank. In this case say, as the spouse, "I charge you, that ye stir not up, nor awake my Love, till he please."[4] Such a rigid severity should you use against the starting of the heart. If Satan should at first cast in a thought of blasphemy, that would make thee quake and shake: therefore, he begins with plausible thoughts. But

---

1 1 Peter 1:13.

2 Psalm 57:7.

3 *"Claudatur contra adversarium pectus, et soli Deo pateat, ne ad se hostem Dei accedere tempore orationis patiatur."*—CYPRIANI *liber De Oratione Dominicâ.*

4 Song of Solomon 3:5.

be careful to observe the first stragglings. Yea, be not diverted by thy very strivings against diversions; and therefore do not dispute with suggestions, but despise them; nor stand examining temptations, but reject them; as blind Bartimeus regarded not the rebukes of the people, but cried the more after Christ; or as travellers do not stand beating back the dogs that bark at them, but hold on their course. This is to be religiously obstinate and severe to our purpose. Satan, contemned, has the less advantage against you. When he is writing images upon the fancy, do not vouchsafe to look upon them. A crier in the court that is often commanding silence, disturbs the court more than they that make the noise; so disputing with our distractions increases them; they are better avoided by a severe contempt.[1]

6. *Bring with you to every holy service strong spiritual affections.*—Our thoughts would not be at such a distance from our work, if our affections were more ready and more earnestly set: it is

---

1 "Besides, the best remedy which you can adopt is strict attention in this duty: if images of things begin to rush in crowds into your mind, you should not only be unconcerned about them, stopping neither to cast them away nor to examine their quality, but you should also comport yourself as though you disdained even to look upon them. For the mere turning aside to those obtrusive thoughts, for the purpose of examining them, is itself an act of wandering; and already has the adversary of our souls extorted something from us, and gained an advantage," etc.—JACOBUS ALVAREZ. *(Nichols' trans.)*

the unwilling servant that is loath to stay long at his work, but is soon gone. Could we bring ourselves more delightfully to converse with God, our hearts would hold our minds close, and we would not straggle so often as we do: therefore, see you do this, or you do nothing. "I was glad," says David, "when they said unto me, Let us go into the house of the Lord."[1] Were we of this frame of spirit, many directions [we] would not need. Now, what should hinder us from being thus affected? Are not the ordinances of God the special means of our communion with him? and the throne of grace, the very porch of heaven? Can we be better than in God's company, pleading with him for our soul's good, and waiting for his blessing? Therefore, let us be glad, and rejoice in his presence; and you will not easily find such out-strayings of mind and thought.

7. *Remember the weight and consequence of the duties of religion.*—That is a cure for slightness. You are dealing with God in a case of life and death; and will you not be serious? With what diligence and earnestness does an advocate plead *with a man*, in a case wherein he himself is not concerned, either for the life of another, or the inheritance or goods of another! And will not you plead earnestly *with God,* when your soul is in danger, when it is a case of eternal life and death, as all matters that

1 Psalm 122:1.

pass between God and us are?[1] Certainly, if we did consider the weight of the business, the heart would be freed from this garish wantonness. If Christ had taken you aside into the garden, as he took Peter, James, and John, and you had seen him praying and trembling under his agonies, you would have seen that it is no light matter to go to God in a case of the salvation of souls, though you have never so much assurance of the issue; for so Christ had. The frequent return of Christian duties makes us to forget the consequence of them. In hearing the Word, be serious; it is your life. "Set your hearts to observe all the words of this law. For it is not a vain thing for you; because it is your life."[2] Thy everlasting estate is upon trial; and the things that are spoken,

---

1 "If when we supplicate a man of exalted rank, I will not say, *for our own life and salvation,* but even *for the purpose of obtaining advantages for some other person,* fastening all the keen sight of our mind's eye as well as that of our body intently upon him, we hang with trembling expectation upon the slightest motion of his countenance, entertaining no small dread lest perchance an indiscreet or inappropriate word should escape from our lips, to avert the flow of mercy from the breast of him who favors us with an audience:—with how much greater ardency, caution, and solicitude, then, ought we to address ourselves as suppliants to Him who takes cognizance of all secrets, while we are engaged before him in deprecating the peril of eternal death, which is impending over us, and to which we are obnoxious!" —CASSIANUS, col. 23. c. 7. *(Nichols' trans.)*

2 Deuteronomy 32:46, 47.

concern your souls. Every act of communion with God, every participation of his grace, has an influence upon eternity. Say, therefore, as Nehemiah in another case, "I am doing a great work, so that I cannot come down."[1] Can you have a heart to mind other things, when you are about so great a work as the saving of your souls?

8. *Let every experimental wandering make you more humble and careful.*—If men did lay their wanderings to heart, and retract them, even every glance with a sigh, the mind would not so boldly, so constantly, digress and step aside. All actions displeasing are not done so readily; therefore, it is good to bewail these distractions. Do not count them as light things. Cassianus, speaking of these wandering thoughts, says, "The most that come to worship, being involved in greater sins, scarce count distraction of thoughts an evil,"[2] and so the mischief is increased upon them. It is a sad thing to be given up to a vain mind, and such a frothy spirit as cannot be serious; therefore; if we do soundly humble ourselves for these offenses, and they did once become *our burden*, they would not be *our practice*.

1 Nehemiah 6:3.
2 "To some who are entangled with vices of the grosser kind, all these wandering thoughts seem to be trivial, and scarcely coming within the verge of sin; but to those who know and value the blessing of perfectness, the multitude even of these very little things is grievous and distressing." —CASSIANUS col. 23. c. 7. *(Nichols' trans.)*

One saith,[1] that huntsmen observe of young dogs, that if a fresh game come in view, they leave their old scent; but if soundly beaten off from it, they kindly take to their first pursuit. The application is easy: did we rate our hearts for this vanity, and pray against the sins of our prayers with deep remorse, this evil would not be so familiar with us.

9. *A constant heavenliness and holiness of heart.*—If men were, as they should be, ἅγιοι ἐν πάσῃ ἀναστροφῇ, "holy in all manner of conversation,"[2] in solemn duties, good and proper thoughts would be more natural and kindly to us. They that live in a constant communion with God, do not find it such a tedious business to converse with him. If they have any excursion of thoughts, it is in their daily work, and the offices of the common life, which they are ever seasoning with some gracious meditations and short ejaculations. When they are in duty, they are where they would be: constant gravity and serious-ness is a great help to them. Men allow themselves a lawless liberty in their ordinary conversations; and then in prayer they know not how to gather up their hearts. Such as men are *out of prayer*, such they will be *in prayer*. We cannot expect that pangs of devotion should come upon us all of a sudden; and that when we come reeking from the world, we should presently leap into a heavenly frame.

1 HOOKER on Acts 2:37.
2 1 Peter 1:15.

10. The next remedy is *frequent, solemn meditation*.—If the understanding were oftener taken up with the things of God, and our thoughts were kept in more frequent exercise, they would the better come to hand. There is a double advantage comes to us by meditation:—

(1.) *The soul gets more abundance of heart-warming knowledge.*—And therefore will not be so barren and dry, which certainly is a cause of wandering. "My heart is inditing a good matter;" and then "my tongue is the pen of a ready writer."[1] A man that boils and concocts truths in his heart, has a greater readiness of words and affections: there is a "good treasure" within him,[2] out of which he may spend freely. One expresses it thus: "He that has store of gold and silver in his pocket, and but a few brass farthings, will more readily, upon every draught, come out with gold and silver than brass farthings: so he that has stocked his heart with holy thoughts, will not find carnal musings so rife and frequent."[3]

(2.) *By use a man gets a greater command over himself.*—When we constantly leave the thoughts at random, and never lay restraints upon them, it is in vain to think we shall keep them in order when we please. Fierce creatures are tame to those that use to command them. Every art is difficult at first, as

1 Psalm 45:1.
2 Matthew 12:35.
3 Cobbett "Of Prayer."

writing, singing, playing upon an instrument; but we get a facility by use and exercise; yea, not only a facility, but a delight in them: and those things that at first we thought impossible, by a little practice grow easy. Certainly, "the way of the Lord is strength to the upright;"[1] and the more we set ourselves to any good thing, the more ready and prepared are we for it.

---

1 Proverbs 10:29.

Made in United States
Troutdale, OR
07/01/2024

20919727R00040